# Old Kingdom of Ancient Egypt

*A Captivating Guide to the Age of the Pyramids and the Egyptian Pharaohs Who Ruled*

# Free Bonus from Captivating History (Available for a Limited time)

Hi History Lovers!

Now you have a chance to join our exclusive history list so you can get your first history ebook for free as well as discounts and a potential to get more history books for free! Simply visit the link below to join.

Captivatinghistory.com/ebook

Also, make sure to follow us on Facebook, Twitter and Youtube by searching for Captivating History.

# Contents

# Introduction – The Beginnings

For thousands of years, few people seemed interested in the Nile River valley, in what we now call Egypt. Climate and geography made it irrelevant.

People wanted to live in the vast region at the top of Africa, stretching from the edge of the Nile valley across to the Atlantic Ocean. Today, it's a desert. But for millennia, it was a rain-fed, fertile, green grassland. It had everything a nomad needed for the good life.

And what a life they had! For example, their rock drawings in an area 600 km from the present Nile show them hunting, milking cows, competing in friendly foot races against each other, and swimming in lakes.

In contrast, on the edge of this bounteous high savannah lay the Nile valley - an inconsequential line of swamps.

Slowly shifting wind patterns and rainfall changes gradually saw the rolling pasturelands overtaken and replaced by the desert. Stone-age artists were forced to migrate to the only remaining reliable supply of water in the valley of the Nile. Fortunately, deep underground movements in the earth's mantle under the northeast corner of Africa tilted the line of swamps and distant inland mountains. Now the water flowed.

It became the world's longest river, running 6,741 km from central Africa and Ethiopia's highlands to the Mediterranean Sea, fed by an enormous basin covering 10 percent of the African continent.

The Egyptian section of this river was 1,480 km long. It flowed through irrigation-reliant desert riverbanks and across its fertile delta, becoming home to settled groups of former nomads. By 4,000 BC, these people were well established there, farming, living in mud-brick homes, maintaining fortifications, burying their dead in elaborate graves, and trading with the commercial networks spreading through the Middle East as far as Afghanistan and the Indus Valley.

As all tribal people do, they formed into warring, independent clusters that eventually combined into two large ones.

One comprised the green, fan-shaped delta region bordering the Mediterranean where farming was easy, and agriculture made the elites wealthy. This area became known as the "Lower Region" (even though it is further north, which we tend to think of as up). Confused? You will often hear the phrase "Lower Region," so look at the river and not the compass; the mouth of the Nile is lower than its headwaters.

The second region was the curved strip of irrigated riverbanks, averaging about 20 km wide, twisting through the desert like a cobra towards today's Sudan. This desert region is called "Upper Egypt," although it is down in the south.

For several hundred years, the people of the delta and the desert riverbanks retained their separate identities, one adapting to the commercial and cultural influences of the nearby Fertile Crescent and the other to the very different opportunities and pressures coming from Africa.

Then in the early Bronze Age, something earthshaking happened. Egypt was unified. Around 3,000 BC, the desert swallowed the delta. Politicians and soldiers of the riverbank region of Upper Egypt grabbed the rich farmlands of the delta and threw a net of controls and administration over both. They had created the world's very first nation-state.

Now rulers could turn the yearly flooding of the Nile (that fertilized the farms) to the advantage of everyone in both regions. A feudal king could call on large groups of people to dig irrigation canals and grow the state's agricultural wealth. With prosperity came budgets for large government buildings, state temples, and monuments. The Egyptian state progressed with calm, forceful confidence – oiled by religion. A brand-new capital city called Memphis was built at the border of the two united regions, near modern Cairo, even though each region's powerful spiritual and administrative centers were still hundreds of kilometers away in opposite directions.

Tangible finds in archaeological sites all over Egypt prove this unification happened. How it came about is less certain. Today, scholars have a nuanced explanation involving elite marriages, a short sequence of powerful kings, steady cultural dominance, and military exploits. But the ancient Egyptians explained it neatly with stories of a hero, a formidable king called Narmer-Menes. And they backed up their tradition by showing him doing this on beautifully carved stone objects, such as the Narmer Palette.

Let's take a moment to describe this important palette – one of the world's most striking ancient treasures. People in the Nile Valley had long been making their cosmetics by grinding pigments on flat stone palettes about the size of a man's hand or even bigger. Master carvers decorated many, and some of those were made to be purely ornamental or commissioned as tiny monuments commemorating an event or person.

This thin piece of dark grey siltstone is 63 centimeters tall, shaped like a shield, and placed in a temple for public viewing. Narmer was exalted as the king of the desert riverbanks who conquered the delta.

On the front, wearing the traditional white crown of the Upper Egyptian ruler, he stands glorious, calm, and gigantic with a club lifted and ready to strike dead a kneeling opponent from the delta region; Lower Egypt. Dead bodies are strewn everywhere. The gods look on and count the victims of this proud, unstoppable warrior king.

The other side is filled with the entwined necks of two mythical leopard-snakes, which perhaps represent a unified Egypt (since lion goddesses were worshiped in the delta and along the desert river banks). Those leopard-snakes create a small circular space where pigments would be ground if it was a functional palette. Of course, the Narmer Palette was only used for propaganda, so the conquering king also appears on this second side. Much smaller here, he is - nevertheless - supreme as he wears the red crown of the delta region he had recently invaded, looking (with satisfaction?) on his dead enemies.

Whether or not Narmer was a real person, something new and significant happened when all the Nile's people were brought into one political unit and held together by military, administrative, cultural, and commercial forces. Today we have the word "nation. Narmer and his associates didn't. Simply conceiving a nation-state was a breathtaking achievement.

Narmer's name heads the standard list of 30 dynasties that ruled Egypt from 3,100 BC for nearly 3,000 years until 332 BC when Alexander the Great took the Nile Valley from Persian influence and made it a key part of his Macedonian kingdom.

The first two dynasties lasted around 450 years. There is little we know for certain about their kings, but, tantalizingly, one may have been a woman named Merneith.

However, we know more at the start of the third dynasty, about 2700 BC. At that time, history suddenly becomes clearer. We now call this the start of Egypt's Old Kingdom, followed by a Middle and then the Late Kingdom. This first kingdom lasted around 500 years, but what the elites and their people accomplished in just the first few decades of this period leaves us amazed. The most magnificent period of Egypt's long history was about to begin.

And it began with death.

# Chapter 1 – Life after Death

Everyone wants to live forever. The Egyptians knew how to do this.

A person's soul would be kept alive for eternity if the physical body was preserved and maintained undisturbed after death, and mourners regularly provided food in the centuries following.

So, the elites went to great lengths and expense to make certain they were properly buried and long supported. From the days of Narmer, members of royal families and their wealthy top officials were embalmed to ensure preservation and buried beneath low, windowless structures made of mud-brick to keep out wild animals and thieves. Later, these came to be called mastabas (from the Arabic word meaning "bench"), and the word is still used.

Indeed, the standard mastaba had the proportions of a bench; just one story high, four times as long as it was wide, roofed over, with sloping sides, painted brilliant white, and perhaps nine meters high. They were oriented north-to-south since Egyptians said this was essential if one was to enter the afterlife. Placed inside were a statue of the dead person and personal effects which might be useful in the afterlife. The embalmed body was placed underneath this structure.

There was also human sacrifice. In the centuries preceding the Old Kingdom, top officials and court retainers were slaughtered at the time of a king's death and buried next to his mastaba so they could serve him in the afterlife. We don't know if they went willingly to their early death; however, we know most Egyptians believed there was an afterlife. The offer of a place in it, forever assisting the king they served on earth, may have been an attractive option to many of those officials. So, it was common to execute dozens of people when the kings were buried, whether persuaded or pressured. King Djet had 318 retainers executed like this!

This gruesome tradition ended with the Old Kingdom, but the mastaba kept developing. By the middle of the Old Kingdom, embalmed bodies were placed in burial pits under a mastaba at the end of sloping tunnels cut deep into the solid bedrock. They also got roomier. Since a dead official needed as many items after life as he had enjoyed during his years of service to the king, mastabas came to have several rooms - all bulging with necessities.

A small chapel might be attached to the mastaba. There, mourners would bring food that professional priests ritually offered to the deceased and then took home to feed their living families. This was a circular system. It maintained the deceased and ensured a priestly class existed and was always there to perform rituals for those dead.

These tombs were almost always built with mud-brick - certainly before the Old Kingdom when engineers and designers were not proficient in large stone buildings. But even in the opening dynasties of our Old Kingdom period, when kings were using stone to construct pyramid tombs for themselves in place of the traditional mastabas, the wealthy elite continued to use mud-brick.

We might think mud is pretty low down on a list of prestigious building materials, but there was nothing modest about a well-situated, brilliantly white, solid mastaba. It would be awe-inspiring to a peasant working on the Nile's banks, gazing toward the Elite-only burial grounds. Imagine seeing this from the high terrace that is the boundary of irrigated land and the beginning of the desert, stretching from the edge of the Nile valley to the Atlantic Ocean. Today even those ruins draw the same response, looming serene and imposing above the heat and hard work in those same fields.

There was one notable exception to mud-brick mastabas. King Khasekhemwy, the father (or perhaps father-in-law) of the man who founded the Old Kingdom and built the first stone pyramid, lined the underground burial chamber of his 58-room mastaba with finished stone.

His son, King Djoser, is thought to have finished that royal mastaba on the death of Khasekhemwy. But even if he did not, the new king had seen what could be done with stone in a mausoleum. When Djoser turned his thoughts to his own burial, the first Old Kingdom king conceived something in stone that stunned the world and still enthralls us.

# Chapter 2 – The First Pyramid

Lists of kings and their rule were first drawn up several thousands of years after the first Egyptian dynasties. Today, they can only be a rough guide because the names and sequence are disputed at many points. An ancient Egyptian "year" is not always our modern 12 months, and each new reign was considered to have begun at Year One. These lists have Djoser coming to power around 2,630 BC, on his father's death. But they also put this son at the head of a new dynasty, the third.

That is strange. A dynasty normally changes when a family line is terminated in a civil war or cannot produce a male heir. But in the lists, the third dynasty is started by a son who inherited the kingdom without overthrowing anyone.

It's also striking. Two millennia after his death, Djoser was still especially valued and pointedly honored by the early historians who drew up the lists.

It's not hard to guess why. Surely these historians gave him this unique prominence in the king lists because Djoser ushered in the glorious Age of the Pyramids. He built the first one, the massive Step Pyramid.

It was the world's first monumental stone building. Djoser built it in the royal graveyard of Saqqara (across the Nile from Memphis, more or less opposite today's Cairo) to house his body and assure him of a place in the afterlife.

It started with much more modest aims; he just wanted a mastaba. But over the next 20 years, it was expanded and redesigned in stages until it was a multi-layered, unconventional structure unlike anything ever seen.

**Djoser's pyramid.**
User:Roweromaniak, CC BY-SA 2.5 PL <https://creativecommons.org/licenses/by-sa/2.5/pl/deed.en>, via Wikimedia Commons
https://commons.wikimedia.org/wiki/File:Sakkara_C02-32.jpg

Actually, from the start, Djoser went rogue with tradition. He and his remarkable architect, the priest of the sun god Re at Heliopolis, Imhotep, began building a square mastaba (not a rectangular one) from small limestone bricks (not mud bricks), eight meters high, 63 meters on each side, finished in quality limestone from Tura, across the river near Memphis, and lining up with the four cardinal points of the compass.

Then they conceived a revolutionary new shape, placing a smaller mastaba on top of the first one. The royal mastaba was no longer a horizontal bench. It now had a component of height – and that gave the design a sense of upward movement.

This design appears to have gripped the imagination of the king and his architect, Imhotep. Even before they had completed this two-tier structure, Djoser directed that more tiers be added on the top, that the base be expanded to become a rectangle measuring 109 by 121 meters, and the whole structure be oriented East to West.

The first mastaba's single-tier had been built conventionally, laying horizontal courses of stone blocks, each slightly larger than conventional bricks. But when it was enlarged with tiers on top, Imhotep ordered that larger stones be used for all the remaining development and placed not horizontally - but leaning inwards towards the center at an angle of 20 degrees. This modification saved significant amounts of stone, so the structure was lighter and safer. Fewer workers were needed, and it gave the outer side of each successive tier a 70-degree slope.

To make room for all the changes in height and floor area, Djoser demolished a small temple adjacent to the first square mastaba. An earlier tunnel to the underground burial chamber was filled in and replaced with another dug from further out. It seemed nothing could restrain the pharaoh's budget, the royal imagination, or the genius of his architect.

Eventually, these two men had built a remarkable new shape - a stack of six mastabas on top of each other, some 330,400 cubic meters of limestone. The sides of each tier were sloping. The whole structure was clad in polished, white limestone. It rose a jaw-dropping 62.5 meters into the desert sky.

Looking at it today, we see a pyramid with jagged sides and a stubby top; a proto-pyramid. It lacks the smooth sides of those true pyramids which developed later. But because each tier was given a specific height and covered a carefully calculated area of the one beneath it (creating sloped sides), this astounding limestone structure has the undeniable look and feel of a pyramid. We agree it was the world's first massive stone pyramid.

To mark the audacity and accomplishment of what they'd done, Djoser carved the name of his architect-priest, Imhotep, next to his own royal name on an imposing stone statue of the king - a statue that all visitors would walk past when approaching the pyramid. Publicly connecting a mere human official with the mighty pharaoh who represented the gods (and at times even morphed into them) was a spectacular honor for Imhotep. It also perhaps reflects Djoser's remarkable willingness to do new things.

Some things could not be changed. The Egyptian religion required that certain traditions were retained. For example, Djoser's burial chamber was at the heart of the design, lined with granite at the bottom of a 28-meter shaft and sealed with a granite plug weighing several tons. Passageways and chambers were needed for family members who might be buried in his tomb. Rooms were built and stocked with the many daily items the king would use in the afterlife. Many of these rooms and passages were decorated with thousands of small turquoise porcelain tiles, apparently matching the decor of the royal rooms Djoser lived in during life.

Djoser's tomb was guarded with a confusing maze of underground tunnels to deter future tomb robbers. Eventually, the burial chamber was found and robbed, although the thieves did leave behind part of the king's mummified foot.

The Step Pyramid stood in 37 acres of reserved land. It was a complex bigger than many towns of the day, holding shrines, priest apartments, and a mortuary temple encircled by a ten-meter-high wall, with a single entrance. There was nothing modest about Djoser's pyramid.

As immutable as it must have seemed when constructed, 4,700 years of weathering, decay, and earthquakes (the latest, a 5.8 magnitude in 1992) brought the world heritage pyramid to the verge of collapse at the turn of the 21st century. In 2006, Egyptian authorities declared an emergency, scrambled to develop a rescue plan with international help, beginning the race to save it.

Then, in 2011, a political revolution swept the country's president from power, and in the confusion that followed, work at the pyramid was forced to a halt. Thieves and intruders broke into the site. Still, preservation efforts restarted, only to run into loud criticism and fears from NGOs and UNESCO that the repair was actually making things worse. Great airbags were inflated to prop up failing chambers. Iron rods were driven into the rock layers to bind sections of stone together. Clever restoration works were completed in the burial chamber and elsewhere.

In 2020, having spent some $6.6 million during those 14 years, all experts accepted the repair, declared it complete, and visitors were again able to visit the remarkable Step Pyramid.

# Chapter 3 – The Second Pyramid

The next attempt at a pyramid followed Djoser's model but was less successful.

The foundations were prepared at Meidum, about 65 km up the river from the Step Pyramid. We don't know with certainty who commissioned it. However, we know from inscriptions it was completed by the first king of the fourth dynasty, Snefru. That ambitious ruler may have been the last of the third dynasty kings, Huni, who came to power some 12 years after Djoser, ruled for about 24 years and built several small step pyramids along the Nile Valley.

We can also trace its development. It started as a step pyramid with seven tiers. Then each of those tiers was made wider and a little higher, and an eighth layer was added as the new top tier. Here was a structure 92 meters tall, built from almost 640,000 cubic meters of rock and with all the outside stones of this grand structure dressed and polished.

**The Meidum pyramid.**
*Zezinho68, CC BY-SA 4.0 <https://creativecommons.org/licenses/by-sa/4.0>, via Wikimedia Commons https://commons.wikimedia.org/wiki/File:Meidum_Pyramid_2.jpg*

A small burial chamber was begun, built into the actual core of the pyramid rather than deep in the foundation rock, as Djoser's was. To place the chamber there, engineers had to find a way to deal with the crushing weight of the stones above. They used corbelling to form an arch over the chamber, which deflected and managed the downward forces inside the structure. Access was through a long sloping tunnel connected to a vertical shaft.

To all appearances, it would seem the project was on track. Not so.

By this time, around 2575 BC, Snefru was the king and had taken over the Meidum pyramid. He was the founder of a new dynasty, the fourth, and no doubt intent on preparing a tomb fit for someone as important as himself. He ordered the steps filled with exceptionally fine limestone and formed into a continuous, smooth slope rising at 53 degrees from the base to a pointed top. From the outside, it would appear he had built a "true" pyramid. However, he had merely added a smooth layer of white stone over an existing, jagged step pyramid.

He had also done something else. The great pioneer Egyptologist, Flinders Petrie, discovered in 1892 that at the base, it was 1100 ancient Egyptian cubits in circumference and 175 cubits high. That is a ratio of 7:44 and required the sides to slope at 51 degrees. These are the exact proportions of the now world-famous Great Pyramid built by Snefru's son, Khufu (also known as Cheops) many years later to the north, on a desert terrace at the edge of modern Cairo.

If this was hubris, the gods punished Snefru. His adaptation fell to pieces; the white layer slid off.

With hindsight, we can see it would never remain in place because the polished stone tiers were not horizontal but sloped slightly to the outside edges. Also, while the original step pyramid was built on solid bedrock, the king's limestone cladding rose up on a foundation of sand. Gravity, time, and the constant attacks by generations of peasants stealing the layer of fine stones doomed it.

Today, all that remains above ground are the cores of three tiers. They stand on a mound of rubble and sand which hides the bottom tiers. What we see is impressive, but this is a pyramid that looks more like a tall knob of stone; it has height but not shape.

Snefru may have witnessed this collapse, but it seems he was not overly concerned if he did. In fact, he might have always intended this pyramid to be a cenotaph rather than his actual tomb because the burial chamber was never finished, no sarcophagus was placed inside, and the traditionally necessary mortuary temple was not completed. Plus, he was already building more pyramids.

Snefru's confidence and sophistication are breathtaking. Rising to power almost 40 years after Djoser was buried in his pro-pyramid at Saqqara, the towering Snefru and his son, Khufu, gave the world the magnificent monuments and magical Old Kingdom culture that have been marveled at for 4,600 years since. This pharaoh shook the world.

# Chapter 4 – The Third Pyramid / Snefru Makes His Statement

Snefru's next pyramid was at Dahshur, some 50 km North of Meidum, close to Djoser's Step Pyramid - and just as visible to the peasant farmers in the fields along the Nile.

From the day the foundation was leveled, it was obvious this pyramid would be big and bold. Eventually, it soared 105 meters into the blue Egyptian sky, using 1.2 million cubic meters of stone. That's twice as much as the Meidum monument -built with twice as much material as Imhotep's construction for Djoser.

However, hubris or the rudimentary engineering knowledge of the day seems to have conspired against Snefru on this building site. His engineers initially had the sides sloping at approximately 60 degrees. That was a problem. When the monument was some 40 meters high, cracks appeared. The catastrophe at Meidum was about to be repeated!

**The Bent Pyramid.**

*GD-EG-Saqqara004.JPG: Néfermaâtderivative work: JMCC1, CC BY-SA 2.5 <https://creativecommons.org/licenses/by-sa/2.5>, via Wikimedia Commons https://commons.wikimedia.org/wiki/File:GD-EG-Saqqara004b.jpg*

A ring of stones was thrown around the base of the pyramid as a sort of belt, lengthening the sides of the square base to almost 189 meters. A new set of casing stones had to be cut and laid up the sides, which changed the slope's angle to around 54 degrees.

Remedial work finished, builders began again, leaning the core stones inwards towards the center as they had done for the first 40 meters - exactly as stones had been laid in the earlier two pyramids. But when they were just nine meters higher, the engineers ordered a completely new specification for the remaining work; stones were now placed in horizontal courses, and the slope was changed to 43 degrees.

This change gave the structure an odd, squat shape, and we now call it the Bent Pyramid. That was not the only highly visible change Snefru made; he also completely redesigned its orientation and the area around it.

As we have seen, the third dynasty's two pyramids were step pyramids, oriented north-south, enclosed in a large rectangular space, with small mastaba tombs of family and officials built nearby. But here, at the start of the fourth dynasty, the Bent Pyramid was new and different. It had a true pyramid shape. Also, it was oriented east-west to face the rising sun in deference to the great god of the sun, falcon-headed Re, who began to dominate Egyptians religion under Snefru. Further, it was walled into a cramped square space, with just three highly significant religious structures carefully placed around it.

The first of these religious structures was a small temple built a few hundred meters to the northeast, where the irrigated river valley gave way to the desert. A small settlement for the priests sprang up around it.

From there, Snefru constructed a broad limestone walkway, with carvings on low sidewalls and ending at a corner of the pyramid. This dramatic feature would lead priests and worshippers from the Land of the Living up to the tomb of their great pharaoh. Then, inside the yellow-grey limestone wall that almost hugged the base of the pyramid, the king constructed a small temple where worshippers could offer gifts and worship.

He built a second, tiny pyramid at the back, and although a pygmy beside the 105-meter-high Bent Pyramid, this second pyramid is more significant. For one thing, it was built from the foundations up with horizontal courses of stone, like the top half of its towering neighbor. This technique had never been exclusively used before and became the way future pyramids were built. Then, a small set of tunnels and a burial chamber were built inside this little pyramid. They were too small to accommodate a person and must have been purely didactic.

Called the "Queen's Pyramid" by later generations, this is a perfect pyramid, constructed in classic proportions and without doubt the model for Snefru's illustrious son, Khufu. He would soon build the Great Pyramid that became one of the Seven Wonders of the ancient world.

Just as the Bent Pyramid's new alignment and subsidiary structures became the model for the royal pyramids built after it, this king brought new models. He mounted successful military campaigns south to Nubia and west into Libya, bringing back loot, slaves, and enough domesticated animals to stock 35 new royal farms in the delta and the large Faiyum Basin near the Bent Pyramid. Tradition presents Snefru as a good king who addressed his subordinates as "friends." Surely this is what any Egyptian ruler would want.

Perhaps this confidence and calmness got him through the shock when his engineers came to him with the bad news of the Bent Pyramid cracks, then later with a plan to bend his pyramid. At any rate, some 49 meters up, when the slope was changed to 43 degrees, he decided it would be merely a cenotaph and ordered work to immediately begin nearby on his third major pyramid, the Red Pyramid.

It appears he was buried in the Red Pyramid, as we will see shortly. However, his cult worship would be maintained for hundreds of years at the Bent Pyramid's valley temple, where the glorious morning sun was welcomed at dawn each day. Worshippers brought food to sustain the pharaoh in the afterlife.

# Chapter 5 – The Red Pyramid: The First True Pyramid

This calm system of methodical ritual and worship was at variance with the intellectual fervor of Snefru and his engineers as they turned their attention to their next project. Their ancestors had conceived and built pyramids in steps, as we have seen. They were little more than high, steep, artificial hills. Indeed, this was how other ancient civilizations in other parts of the world erected their pyramids. In the Nile Valley, this king and his engineers conceived the abstract geometrical form of a massive true pyramid and set about to build it.

This undertaking was a remarkable conception intellectually, a huge reputational and financial gamble, and a testament to perseverance and outstanding project management by a technical team that had attempted this before and failed twice. Snefru was in a race pitting engineering ideas against time.

**The Red Pyramid.**

*jokertrekker, CC BY 3.0 <https://creativecommons.org/licenses/by/3.0>, via Wikimedia Commons https://commons.wikimedia.org/wiki/File:The_Red_Pyramid,_Saqqara_-_panoramio.jpg*

Workers thoroughly tested the ground on a new site close to the Bent Pyramid and laid a square base with sides 220 meters long. Taking their cues from the pygmy pyramid next to the Bent Pyramid, they laid the reddish, iron-rich limestone core stones in horizontal courses. They cut white, high-quality Tura limestone casing stones to slope upwards at 43 degrees.

Hidden inside at the end of tunnels, they left three chambers, each vaulted with a system of corbels that still successfully bear the two million tons of rock around and above them. Partial remains of a mummy were found in one by early archaeologists and seemed to indicate Snefru was laid to rest here. However, his worship was conducted two kilometers away at the Bent Pyramid, as we have seen.

Most of the Tura casing stones were torn out in the Middle Ages and used for buildings in Cairo, but on the back of some of those which remain, we have found dates recorded by workmen. These show it took two years to lay the first six layers of stone, but some 30 percent of the entire structure was finished two years later. It is possible that the whole structure was completed in 17 years.

It towered 105 meters into the air, a true pyramid shape, sides polished and gleaming white. It must have made an enormous impact at the time, and its harmonious form still captivates us today. However, what happened next was so astounding it managed to eclipse even this breathtaking achievement.

# Chapter 6 – The Great Pyramid

One of Snefru's younger sons, Khufu, had undoubtedly been taking notes as he grew up watching his father master the new pyramid form as he built the two at Dahshur. He succeeded his father as a young man of 25 or 30 years and quickly gave directions to survey and test a rocky plateau of solid rock 20 kilometers to the north, overlooking the Nile River at Giza. Would it be suitable for his own pyramid tomb?

His engineers gave it the thumbs up. Khufu rolled up his royal sleeves and 4,600 years ago began to build the Seventh Wonder of the ancient world that today we call the Great Pyramid.

**The Great Pyramid.**

*Nina R from Africa, CC BY 2.0 <https://creativecommons.org/licenses/by/2.0>, via Wikimedia Commons https://commons.wikimedia.org/wiki/File:Giza_Pyramid_Complex_(46845616672).jpg*

The site chosen included a small solid rise. It was left in place, with flat terraces cut across it to seat sections of the first layers of core rocks that would soon arrive on the site.

However, the perimeter of the 13-acre square pyramid base was leveled with great precision. The 230-meter sides are horizontal to within 21 millimeters (a touch more than half an inch), and the length of each of them at the long base varies by an average of only 58 millimeters (under 2-1/2 inches.) The four right angles at the corners are accurate to within one part in 10,000, and the whole thing is oriented with the four cardinal points. From this base, the four smooth sides slope up at an angle of 51 degrees. All this was done with rudimentary bronze and wood tools; no iron, no wheels or pulleys, and to a standard about as good as a modern engineer would achieve with lasers.

Khufu's engineers had learned from his father's designers that placing the stones in horizontal layers is the optimum technique for building the perfect pyramid. They laid the stones on the Giza plateau this way, placing large, heavy stones in the bottom courses (close to 1 ½ meters - or five feet - high), progressively placing smaller, lighter stones higher up until the layers near the top were only about 50 centimeters tall (about 18 inches.) Inside this mountain of stone, workers constructed a network of passages, some puzzling, narrow shafts, three impressive chambers, and a sarcophagus carved from a single large granite block. It rose a staggering 146.5 meters (480 feet) when they had finished—a world record that stood for the next 3,811 years until Lincoln Cathedral was completed 14 meters (46 feet) higher.

It is estimated some 2.3 million limestone blocks were needed for Khufu's pyramid. The core stones came from a source of yellow-grey stone just south of the pyramid site, having an average weight of 2.5 tons. Most were never intended to be seen, so they were only roughly dressed, with gypsum mortar and small stones between them where necessary to fill in gaps and stop them from moving. A smaller number were on view or were used as backing for the precision-cut casing stones - their sides smoothed with great care. Those casing stones were cut and shaped from high-quality white limestone from the well-used quarries at Tura, 10 kilometers away on the other side of the river.

Also, there were 8,000 tons of granite blocks used for lining and strengthening the interior chambers. These were floated down the Nile River to Giza from Aswan, 860 kilometers away. Some of those granite stones weighed nearly 80 tons! Add 500,000 tons of mortar to all this, and we have a structure weighing something like 5.75 million tons. It's a testament to the foundation engineers and master stonemasons that the pyramid did not break the ground it stood on or that the interior chambers and lower layers have not shifted and slowly collapsed.

Moving all this material up to the Giza plateau demanded organization of the highest order. Khufu inherited those abilities from his father, who also needed project managers and bureaucrats to oversee and complete his giant pyramid projects. They had developed the skills and systems to do this, and their sons and apprentices worked for Khufu, maintaining a steady supply of stones to the engineers directing work on top of the Khufu's slowly rising structure.

We know about one of them, called Merer. He supervised men on the other side of the river and (presumably by accident) left behind one of his papyrus logbooks in a Tura quarry, found in 2013. It has fascinating details of food supplies for his work gangs, quantities of finished stone shipped to the building site on certain days, what quarters he slept in each night, and so on.

The rock cutters themselves also recently came into clearer view when archaeologists discovered a rock quarry used in Khufu's time. At this quarry, partly excavated stone blocks and a complete set of ancient wooden mallets, stone tools, and bronze chisels left where workers had placed them 4,600 years ago.

Using this time capsule as a guide, a French stonemason demonstrated that a team of four men could use those tools to cut out a 2.5-ton block of limestone suitable for the pyramid's core in six hours. An American stonemason experimented elsewhere and got roughly similar results.

These investigations give us clues to the conditions and workloads under which the ancient quarrymen worked. Even so, we are left speechless when considering a later generation of workers equipped with the same gear who cut, dressed, and moved a 200-ton limestone block to the mortuary temple of Khufu's grandson, Menkaure.

The centerpiece of Khufu's project was the pyramid. But ritual and religion demanded several other vitally important structures that seem inconsequential ruins today. They included a small temple built some 40 meters lower down than the pyramid, to the northeast, where the Nile River is thought to have run at the time of Khufu. Priests would have had their homes near it, and, likely, a busy port was also located there, receiving streams of people, supplies, and rock.

That temple was connected by a long causeway running up to the pyramid. On the southern side of this walkway, the royal family and elite officials built mastaba tombs for themselves, laid out in orderly rows. Where the causeway ended at the pyramid itself, a mortuary temple was incorporated into a perimeter wall that hugged the giant tomb. Only the basalt floor of that temple remains, but the complex was spread over an area of some 50 by 40 meters. Here, worshippers came to offer food that would sustain the pharaoh in his afterlife and then be used to feed the priests and their families in this life.

Nearby, there's a line of four 30-meter-high stone pyramids. Three still stand, but so little of the fourth remains that it was unknown until traces of the foundation were discovered recently by accident. Their purpose is obscure. However, one thing is clear; the whole complex is oriented east to west - exactly how Snefru had laid out his pyramids. This tells us that Khufu had adopted the religious emphasis of his father and was giving due prominence to the falcon-headed sun god

Re. This great complex looked to the east, where the sun rose every day.

But there were special items that were deliberately kept hidden from the sun. They were wooden boats, perhaps six or seven of them, buried underground in unmarked stone pits.

Most of these boat pits were opened and emptied in antiquity. But two untouched pits were discovered buried in sand in 1954 by an Egyptian archaeologist doing some menial work along the line where the pyramid's perimeter wall once stood.

The first was carved out of bedrock, roofed with 41 massive, five-meter-long limestone slabs weighing almost 20 tons each, and made airtight with pitch. To everyone's amazement and thrill, inside was a pile of rope and wooden planks, the components of a fully functional ancient boat made from Lebanese cedar and acacia that had been carefully dismantled and stored in 1,200 pieces when Khufu built his pyramid.

It took 14 years of research and careful work to reassemble it, but the most magnificent ship emerged from the pile of twisted, dangerously fragile planks and old rope. It was 44 meters long, nearly six meters wide, with a displacement of about 45 tons and a draft of 1.5 meters. The shape and proportions of this elegant vessel are spellbinding. If launched into the Nile today, it would be seaworthy.

The pharaoh may have used it on the Nile during his lifetime or to ferry his body on his final journey to the pyramid. On the other hand, it might have been intended to ferry Khufu to the afterlife as a solar barque.

The next boat pit presented a near-insurmountable problem. The wooden vessel was also carefully dismantled, but the seal between the 20 large covering slabs had leaked, and the resulting humidity and heat inside had all but destroyed the ancient timbers by 1987 - when experts first peered in. However, after 12 years of strenuous international conservation effort, each piece of the boat's wood has been preserved and made robust, and the vessel is being reassembled.

How long all the components of this pyramid project took to complete is debated by experts today. However, they all agree Snefru's building legacy was passed on to exactly the right man. Khufu and his engineers gave the world a structure that still inspires wonder in everyone who stands next to it for the first time. This achievement has never been matched - although Khufu’s Old Kingdom successors tried.

# Chapter 7 – The Next Three Pyramids

## Djedefre

Khufu's son, Djedefre, was the next ruler, and he made the first attempt to outdo his father.

Djedefre chose a site for his pyramid tomb north of his father's. He dug a trench in the bedrock on a small hill eight kilometers beyond the Giza plateau, shaped this into an access tunnel and a single burial chamber, then built his pyramid over it. That was clever; it gave him a place for his sarcophagus (which may have been made from a block of pink granite) without the difficult, time-consuming work of tunneling under or into the great limestone blocks of his tomb.

He made another even more significant change; he oriented his pyramid complex north to south, not east to west as his father had done. The causeway came to the complex from the north, and an outer perimeter wall was aligned from north to south.

In other respects, Djedefre was religiously conventional. He buried a royal boat next to his tomb, built a mud-brick mortuary temple, and erected small ritual pyramids. Also, he was the first pharaoh to use the title "Son of Re" and link his formal name with the traditional worship of the sun god. Later kings followed his example.

He made his pyramid's base 106 meters long and gave the sides a slope of 51 degrees; his pyramid only reached 67 meters into the air. This was less than half the height of his father's, but a pyramid for the

Son of Re was always going to stir up awe, and no doubt it impacted his people.

**Pyramid of Djedefre.**
*Jon Bodsworth, Copyrighted free use, via Wikimedia Commons*
https://commons.wikimedia.org/wiki/File:Pyramid_of_Djedefre_01.jpg

Those who came later responded differently. Somewhere in antiquity, plunderers carted away most of the stones and casing to make their own buildings. Today the once majestic structure looks like a long heap of rubble.

Robbers were kinder to Khufu's other son.

## Khafre

Khafre, Djedefre's brother, followed as the next pharaoh and set about building his pyramid on the Giza plateau.

As with all Old Kingdom rulers, the dates of his reign are unclear. We know little of his life or political accomplishments. However, it appears he was unwilling to build a small pyramid even though the available space was limited.

He laid the foundation only 190 meters from the Great Pyramid. Still, by excavating bedrock on the northwest corner and building up the opposite southeast corner with massive stone blocks, he built a pyramid measuring 215 meters along the side at the base and stood 136 meters high. This was only a few meters lower than Khufu's, and from some angles, it seemed taller because it rose from a starting point on the bedrock 10 meters higher than the Great Pyramid.

**Pyramid of Khafre.**

*kallerna, CC BY-SA 4.0 <https://creativecommons.org/licenses/by-sa/4.0>, via Wikimedia Commons https://commons.wikimedia.org/wiki/File:The_Sphinx_and_Pyramid_of_Khafre.jpg*

Significantly, the slope of the sides was 53 degrees. That is a little steeper than Khufu's (it angled up at 51 degrees), which made the total mass of Khafre's pyramid considerably less than his father's. That gave him important construction and cost advantages.

Like earlier pharaohs, Khafre sourced the hundreds of thousands of two-ton blocks for his pyramid from nearby limestone quarries. Unlike earlier engineers, however, little care went into laying down these stones in their courses. The layers were often not horizontal.

Frequently, joints are alarmingly wide. Some of the roughly-dressed stones have no mortar between them. But more tellingly, the angles at the corners were not lined up correctly, requiring a small but noticeable correction at the very top.

The same imprecision is visible on the smooth sides, which were cased along the lower layers with pink granite from faraway Aswan, and further up with white limestone from the Tura quarries. There are tiny gaps in many of the joints where limestone casing stones abut each other. But this imperfect workmanship didn't deter later builders who needed some stone. Ramesses II, for example, plundered sections of Khafre's cladding for one of his temples.

Much still remained in 1646 when Oxford University's then professor of astronomy, John Greaves, wrote that the casing was smooth though the stones were smaller and less well laid than those on Khufu's pyramid. But eventually, all was carted off except a patch at the top.

Inside, Khafre adopted a style of "less is more." There is just one plain burial chamber, oriented east to west and roofed with great limestone slabs, a small side chamber for storage, and two straightforward access passages. His designers got the aesthetics right; it is a simplicity that satisfies.

Outside, he ordered pomp and ceremony. The temples and causeway of this pyramid complex combine eye-catching design with size. They are the finest of all remaining Old Kingdom funerary temples. And then there is the mysterious sphinx resting next to Khafre's valley temple at the bottom of the sloping causeway running up from the river to the looming royal tomb of the Son of Re.

The first component of this whole east-west complex is the valley temple, just below the plateau. It is large, on a square plan, with a wide, paved terrace in front. Worshippers entered through either of two doorways into a hall, turning to the main part of the building – a set of three enclosed corridors formed from enormous stone columns weighing up to 150 tons each and housing a dramatic collection of tall stone statues of the pharaoh Khafre. The walls and columns were lined with polished pink granite from Aswan, and the floor was paved with white alabaster. Natural light filtered in from a row of openings high above. To one side was a set of storage rooms, and on the roof, there were facilities for the priests.

A covered causeway, lined with the same pink granite, gave worshippers access to a second temple 46 meters away, up on the plateau at the pyramid's base. This was the mortuary temple where offerings were left to support the pharaoh in his afterlife. In ruins today, it was built on a rectangular plan with storerooms, pillared halls, corridors, stone statues of the pharaoh, an open courtyard, and niches for cult offerings – all lined with highly decorated polished granite and alabaster. This busy building set the pattern for mortuary temples for generations to come.

Boat pits have been uncovered around this top temple; these were, unfortunately, looted in antiquity and are now empty. There are also remains along the southern side of the causeway, perhaps tombs for the specially privileged elite of Khafre's court who won permission to be buried that close to their pharaoh.

## The Sphinx

Then there is the Sphinx. The enigma of Egypt. A riddle lying in plain view. One of the oldest and largest sculptures ever carved anywhere in the world – and probably the most mysterious.

It is 73 meters (240 feet) long, standing 20 meters (66 feet) tall, lined up east to west, directly in line with Khafre's pyramid and next to that pharaoh's valley temple. Who carved this imposing wonder – and why – is disputed.

The mainstream opinion gives Khafre the sponsor's credit since it is aligned with his pyramid and sits next to his valley temple and causeway. Some voices argue for earlier rulers, saying, for instance, it must have been earlier because erosion on the body was caused by rainfall of a type last seen in the Nile valley in 6000 BC when it was a swamp on the edge of savannah lands.

As for the why, theories range from dull to bizarre. Some say the Sphinx and the pyramids collected energy from the sun or that the Sphinx, the pyramids, and the Nile River match a special alignment of stars. No one has yet found undisputed evidence to explain the Sphinx, so we are left with questions.

Here we have a great lion with the head of a man that's sprawled out, paws reaching forward, carved from a hillock of bedrock, its own small temple in front of it. Traces of pigment suggest it was originally lavishly covered with paint. We can safely assume the craftsmanship was breathtaking and lifelike because that's what we find in royal statues on the Giza plateau and in Nile Valley temples. Ancient Egypt's sculptors had absolutely nailed the art of realism in stone.

Their successors can't claim that. In the 1920s, sand that had long-buried parts of the Sphinx was completely removed and restoration work done. Alarmingly, this damaged the iconic headdress, face, and neck! Attempts to correct that only weakened the limestone, and a 315 kg block dropped off the shoulder in 1988.

And Napoleon's cannons? The ones that shot away the Sphinx's nose when the French conquered Egypt? It's the story every schoolchild hears but is completely wrong. Twenty-two years before Napoleon was born, a visiting French artist sketched the sphinx and had no nose.

One question remains unanswered. Among all the texts found on the Giza plateau, there is no mention of the great Sphinx that today dominates its eastern edge. For thousands of years, no writers mentioned the Sphinx, not even the Greek historian Herodotus who, in 440 BC, speculated and commented in detail on the Giza pyramids during his visit to Egypt.

## Menkaure

With Khafre buried, succession may have briefly gone to a minor son, but it was then taken by Khafre's other son, Menkaure, who ruled for about 20 years. (As always, dynastic dates are difficult to verify.)

He continued the tradition of burial in a pyramid but was content with a small one, just 103 meters (339 feet) along the base and sloping up at 51 degrees to a height of only 65 meters (215 feet). It was a well-proportioned structure, with the bottom layers cased in pink Aswan granite and those above in Tura limestone.

**Pyramid of Menkaure.**

*David Broad, CC BY 3.0 <https://creativecommons.org/licenses/by/3.0>, via Wikimedia Commons https://commons.wikimedia.org/wiki/File:Pyramid_of_Menkaure_at_Giza_-_panoramio.jpg*

Inside, there is a complex set of passages and chambers leading to a granite-lined burial chamber. A wonderful basalt sarcophagus was found and removed by early 19th century archaeologists. To their credit, a detailed drawing of it was made before it was shipped off to Europe in 1838. That's all we now have, as the ship carrying it sunk off Malta!

The pyramid's small base had given Menkaure's engineers plenty of options on the rocky plateau. They placed his tomb a comfortable 250 meters away from his father's. This meant its valley temple could be built precisely due east. And as a result, the long causeway connecting it to the mortuary next to the pyramid would emphasize a perfect east to west orientation for the entire complex.

It seems Menkaure intended to emphasize the temples here, just as his father and the later Old Kingdom rulers did. They honor Hathor, the sun god Re, and Horus, whom Menkaure embodied during his lifetime.

Inside the valley temple, the king placed stone statues of himself with the gods and his queen. When they were unexpectedly discovered in the winter of 1910, they stunned the watching world. Several were near life-sized and are among the most sublime ever found in Egypt, exuding haunting beauty, naked power, and serene calm.

In one statue of the king and his queen, the pharaoh stands dressed in a light kilt, youthful, strong, and upright. Here is an individual with prominent eyes, full lips, and rounded nose and cheeks. Menkaure deliberately avoided the formal portrait almost all other pharaohs commissioned for their statues. Similarly, his queen is carved as a specific person, while at the same time, her thin, clinging dress and voluptuous shape are ideal. Without emotion, the couple stands together, gazing into the distance and past.

But he did die and rather suddenly. His pyramid complex was never fully completed in his lifetime.

With its large courtyard and an offering hall on an upper level, only some walls are stone in the valley temple. The rest are mud-brick, evidence that a son completed this religiously important building. Surprisingly, it was eventually taken over by squatters. Archaeologists have found the remains of a village right up at the entrance and evidence of small homes inside the courtyard itself.

Even that magnificent king and queen statue went unfinished. The sculptor achieved a surface on most of the dark stone that amazes us – mirror-smooth and without blemish – but the lower legs don't have their final polish, and no names were inscribed on the base.

The causeway of quality flagstones and mud-brick walls is also half-built, as was the mortuary temple, although that square building began with permanence in mind. A monstrous 200-ton block of local limestone was put into one corner. A heavier one has never been found. And pink Aswan granite slabs were stacked up outside, ready to line the temple interior. They remain there, unused.

# Chapter 8 – The Workers

So, here we have four immense, awe-inspiring structures with their temples and causeways, three on the Giza plateau and another a little north, built by hand about 4,500 years ago by several generations of one family - over a period of barely 80 years. We have no idea how they managed this!

The ancient Greeks thought they knew. About 440 BC, some 2,100 years after the Great Pyramid was completed, their historian, Herodotus, toured the Giza plateau. Greeks ruled Egypt at that time. Because they had local knowledge and contacts, Herodotus believed it when they told him the causeway and Khufu's pyramid had been constructed in 30 years by 100,000 reluctant, slave-like conscripts, fed on bread, onions, leeks, and radishes, toiling in three-month shifts, using short timbers and special machines to pass heavy stones from one layer up to the next.

Today, experts are no further ahead than Herodotus regarding how the stones were lifted into place. Plenty of explanations have been touted, many involving ramps. None has been widely accepted in the archaeological community.

However, there is agreement that Herodotus' depiction of huge rotating armies of near-slaves is a fantasy. For one thing, fewer men could have done the job; perhaps as few as 25,000. There's a growing consensus that 5,000 permanent professionals and around 4,000 short-term, unskilled laborers would have been needed, supported by maybe 16,000 to 20,000 artisans providing food, making and repairing tools, building ramps, bringing in supplies, making mortar, and so on.

Also, archaeologists have uncovered the remains of towns where the builders lived. Inscriptions and graffiti indicate the men who built for Khafre and Menkaure lived in these towns. In the lowest levels, there is some evidence that Khufu's builders also lived there before them. So, just a few feet under the desert sand (within view of the pyramids), we have what we need to learn how a unique industry was manned and run. We now can estimate how many builders there were, know what they ate, see the state of their health, and understand what the pharaoh thought of them.

These were planned settlements nestled against the rock outcrop of the Giza plateau with straight paved streets, drains, public facilities, and standard houses. One township was three square kilometers in area. There seem to be two classes of these towns. Their cemeteries correspond to how we now think the pyramid workforce was organized: professionals, semi-skilled workers, and casual laborers brought in to do the heavy lifting for months at a time from their farming villages. A pharaoh could command labor.

The professionals were designers, carpenters, masons, toolmakers, pyramid decorators, priests, administrators, etc., with titles such as Overseer of Masonry and Inspector of Craftsmen. Their homes were comfortable. Their wives wore wigs, and servants helped them grind and sift wheat for cooking. They wore dresses with beaded collars, lavish necklaces, colored bracelets, leather sandals, and some went bare-breasted. Women were priestesses. There were dwarf women, perhaps performing as entertainers. These people ate bread and cakes, vegetables such as onions, figs and lentils, beef, sheep, pork, fish, and enjoyed beer and wine.

The seasonal laborers were paid in food: ten loaves of bread and beer each day. They were put into groups of around 2,000, then divided into work gangs with names like "Drunkards of Menkaure" and "The white crown of Khnum Khufu is powerful" (Khnum-Khufu was Khufu's full birth name.) Each gang was split into around 200, and those units were divided into clusters of about 20 workers. In this way,

20,000 men on the plateau could be quickly and efficiently put to work exactly where and when they were needed. Even Khufu's gigantic project suddenly looks manageable and achievable. The Egyptian state knew how to harness its people.

These workers seem to have lived in men-only barracks. Long buildings, open on one side and possibly two-storied, have been found in the towns – probably the world's first institutional buildings. Meals were cooked in them, and young village men might have considered these places very adequate sleeping quarters on the hot nights. Merer, the supervisor who lost his logbook in a Tura quarry, records sleeping one night at a time in various places. Perhaps in one of those quarters. There is also a suggestion some workers might have camped in the open nearer the pyramid they were building.

We assume the laborers were well fed because they had the strength to complete those massive projects. It's estimated this heavy work would have required 45 to 50 grams of protein each day. If half of the protein need was met with beans (still popular today in Egypt), lentils, and fish, the rest would need to come from red meat like cattle, sheep, and goats. It did. Archaeologists have uncovered the butcher shops.

Unsurprisingly, most of the excavated animal bones found discarded around shops in the professional areas of the towns were from cattle, the preferred meat. At the barracks, we see the bones of the less prestigious sheep and goats. It is estimated that on days when the work was in full swing, butchers would need to produce some 1,800 kilograms (4,000 pounds) of meat. The farmland necessary for a regular meat supply amounts to five percent of the current land area along the Nile River. Again, we salute the ability of the Old Kingdom administrators to supply this much food month after month for decades.

Building a pyramid did more than promote the state worship of the sun god, Re, and satisfy the king with an eye-catching tomb. It also changed the life of the builders. Imagine a young man leaving his tiny village of, say, 50 homes to work with 15,000 or even 20,000 people he didn't know. He would return months later well fed, with a cosmopolitan outlook, a wider view of what Egypt was, new ideas about life, perhaps some training in a trade or an offer to learn a profession. DNA studies show the workers were Egyptians, not foreigners, so this social and economic impact would have been noticed along the length of the Nile. It harmonized the nation.

When men died on the project, some were buried about a kilometer south of the Great Pyramid rather than back in their villages. In ancient Egypt, this was a great privilege, being buried near the king for whom they had toiled. The elites of their day, Khufu and Khafre's relatives were similarly interred close to the king in expensive mastabas at the causeway and to the West of the Great Pyramid. And here, common people were given the same high honor, although their tombs were much more modest.

Their skeletons lie in burial shafts lined with mud-brick, respectfully curled up and oriented to the east. The men were not mummified (a ritual reserved for the super-rich) but were surrounded by bread and beer provisions for the afterlife. All this reminds us they were not slaves. Here are men who had worked willingly and in death were given dignity and the religious rites of free people.

Dead men do tell tales, of course. Their skeletons speak about how they lived and died. Some show signs of arthritis and abnormal bony growths. Almost all of them show tooth decay and wear. The lower vertebrae on many were damaged. Legs or arms were broken in some. There are signs of accidents and a life of hard labor.

We also find some bones healed with splints, suggesting a health care system in the worker towns. Nevertheless, the average age of these men was around 35 years, rather than the 55 years to which many elites lived. Sadly, in the group of people who died under 30, women and children are overrepresented. The skeleton of a female dwarf has been found; tragically, she had died trying to deliver a normal-size full-term fetus. Childbirth has always been hazardous.

When Menkaure died and was buried in the smallest pyramid on the Giza plateau, the throne was taken by Shepseskaf, who completed Menkaure's temple complex. Little is known about this successor. He may have been Menkaure's son and might have been the last king of this Fourth Dynasty. There's no agreement on how long he ruled, although it was only a few years. He was buried in a simple mastaba tomb South of Giza, at Saqqara.

The Pyramid Age had ended. For 180 years or so - depending on how royal reigns are calculated - generations of two families had conceived, developed, and perfected the pyramid. They left behind eight monuments that came to define ancient Egypt and are all that most of us today learn about the Old Kingdom.

The pharaohs came to be seen as living gods at the top of a social pyramid. Their survival into the afterlife determined eternity for their people, who worshipped and provided for them long after each king had been laid to rest in their massive granite sarcophagus.

Each king held the nation together. His relatives and trusted officials became senior regional administrators and ensured resources flowed to him from along the Nile and the Sinai desert. From them came some of the best engineering minds and most accomplished artists. The third and fourth dynasties spanned a lavish, golden period.

# Chapter 9 – The Fifth Dynasty

There is debate about the fifth dynasty, as its first pharaoh may have been related to the ruling family of the fourth dynasty. Nevertheless, the king lists drawn up much later make this division, and we can see this fifth dynasty is different from the fourth. It lasted around 140 years.

During this time, Egypt's religion came to be expressed differently. The sun god, Re, was given more prominence. For example, pharaohs incorporated his name into theirs by adding titles like "Son of Re" or "Sun King" to their long formal names.

Solar temples were built, featuring the obelisk. It is thought that six were built, mostly at Abusir, but only fragments of two have been discovered. Like the pyramids on the Giza plateau, these sun temples approached a valley temple along a causeway. But inside the temple, proper worshippers found themselves in a large open courtyard, paved with polished basalt and lined with red granite columns, looking up at a tall obelisk that would catch the morning sun rising in the East. Further inside, worshippers could offer food and gifts to support the dead pharaoh and sustain the priests who maintained his cult.

Fifth dynasty kings continued to be buried in pyramids, but these tombs were less imposing than earlier ones, rising up just 50 meters or so. Today, they have all collapsed into ruin. Rulers gave much more time and attention to decorating the temples at the base of these pyramids, lavishing money on sculptures and painters who did magnificent work on the interior walls.

We see this new emphasis in the second king in the dynasty, Sahure. He built his pyramid at Abusir on a base 79 meters long with a slope of 50 degrees. It rose just 47 meters, but one corner is 1.5 meters too long, so adjustments were needed higher up. It was sheathed in white limestone. The internal passageways and burial chamber were wrecked in antiquity when plundered for the granite that lined them.

His valley temple has also disappeared, but fragments of the walls remain. These are decorated with some of the finest examples of relief from the Old Kingdom. On them, the pharaoh is striking down foreigners. He comes face-to-face with the gods and receives great quantities of offerings and gifts. His soldiers are carved and painted with rippling muscles and individual faces, and a fleet of his ships is moored nearby.

From this temple, a once-covered causeway runs 235 meters up to the pyramid, and an impressive mortuary temple kept well-drained with a complicated network of copper drainage pipes. The temple was partly roofed with corridors flanked by ornate columns, the ceilings carved with stars. On walls, the king is shown hunting birds and desert game, his court parades, and he stands over defeated foreign enemies. There are alabaster floors, granite cladding on walls, and a massive false door at the side of the pyramid itself in the spacious offering hall. These doors were possibly originally sheathed with copper or gold, through which the spirit of the dead pharaoh would come to receive the offerings left on a stone altar.

In its day, this splendid temple must have bolstered a worshipper's faith and been bursting with reminders of abundant life. It became the model in size and complexity for many other mortuary temples that followed.

Another change was underway in this fifth dynasty. Power began to devolve to regional governors and officials. They were no longer drawn exclusively from the royal family; they could be sons of the elite. These governors became wealthy. (Of course!) We see this in their mastabas which got bigger, contained wonderful statues of themselves, and were decorated in a new style showing scenes from a generous Nile valley that would provide for them in the great expanses of the afterlife. As we shall see, this administrative change and its consequences were to have a mortal impact on the pharaohs' powers.

Towards the end of the dynasty, faith again shifted. Re, the great and powerful sun god, was supplanted by a new god, Osiris, lord of the underworld.

For centuries, Egyptians had believed their pharaoh was a son of Re and that the king joined Re in the afterlife. Tomb texts by the end of the fifth century were giving them an alternative. Pharaohs from then on were associated with Osiris, and just as green-skinned Osiris rose from death in the deity’s myths, so the king would pass into life with him and become immortal - with the right magic.

By the end of the dynasty, almost all Egyptian tombs carried a prominent mention of Osiris. None more so than the pyramid of the fifth dynasty's last ruler, Unas. Its walls are covered with magic spells and written references to Osiris and the beliefs about eternity associated with him.

Spells and arcane knowledge of the afterlife failed Unas in the end. He never had a son. His dynasty broke!

# Chapter 10 – The Sixth Dynasty

The transition to another ruling line was made by a man called Teti. He may have been Unas' son-in-law; however, he took over around 2323 BC and founded the sixth dynasty, which was to last about 175 years.

This switch seems to have been smooth because Teti retained senior officials from the former court. He married a daughter to an adviser who later became a leading priest. Sometime after, he gave tax exemptions to the temple of Osiris and Isis at Abydos. These actions suggest the elite bureaucrats and clerics were strong, perhaps even more in charge of affairs than Teti, and initially felt their pharaoh would fit in with a new balance of power emerging along the Nile.

Upon Teti's death, the next succession was rough. His son, Pepi, did not immediately succeed his father. Rather, the prince had to wait for the end of the one-year reign of a shadowy intermediary. Some suggest this other person was put onto the throne by powerful, non-family elites who lost out to the true heir, Pepi, after several months of struggle. We do not know, but we can imagine this drama was possible given the normal dynamics of dynastic change and the growing power of the regions.

Pepi struggled against officials and priests for much of his 40-year reign. Towards the end, he may have even discovered one of his wives was plotting against him. He managed to stay ahead by taking action in the regions and quickly rotating officials through regional posts. He spent money on local cult temples as a benefactor. Also, he built a regional network of special cult centers dedicated to the worship of himself. He recruited local non-elites to small regional positions to counter powerful traditional local families and reorganized royal farmlands to make collecting taxes and labor easier. He maximized a flourishing international trade. He married into the family of a powerful governor of Abydos in Upper Egypt, which gave him influence within that family and gave the governor access and privilege in the pharaoh's inner circles. And interestingly, in light of something recorded in the tomb of his grandson, Pepi II, he gave tax exemptions to two towns adjacent to the Bent Pyramid of Snefru.

Pepi prepared for his death by authorizing a pyramid complex at Saqqara that fitted the now-standard formula: the pyramid itself (only 52 meters high), a simple burial chamber inside it, and temples at each end of a causeway. Pepi's pyramid passages and burial chamber walls are covered with statements and magic spells written in green hieroglyphs arranged in over 2,000 columns. At the end of the fifth dynasty, Unas had done this before him on a much smaller scale. After Pepi, each Old Kingdom pharaoh filled his pyramid walls with text.

A son took the throne briefly after him, then his six-year-old grandson, Pepi II, came to power.

During the time of Pepi II, the Sinai continued to be mined for precious minerals, trade with the Levant thrived, caravans went down to Nubia and came back with ivory, incense, ebony, and, on at least one occasion, a dancing dwarf. News of the capture of the pygmy filtered back to the court when Pepi II was a boy. He wrote an excited letter to the head of the caravan assuring him of a sizable reward if the dwarf could be kept alive and shown to the young king. A copy of the letter was found in the tomb of that caravan official.

There is debate about the length of his rule. Ancient king lists give Pepi II a highly improbable 94 years. A consensus has more recently formed around 64. We can say it was long enough for the state to ossify and central power diminish. Regional governors were not taxed, and their positions were now being handed down to sons. Thus, for several generations, they and other regional families became strong and increasingly took opportunities to extend their strength. Power flowed steadily out to the regions.

When Pepi II died, the Old Kingdom quickly collapsed into independent, warring fiefdoms. Egypt found itself back where it started about 1,000 years earlier, with the ordinary people of the Nile valley at the mercy of warlords and praying for another Narmer-Menes. It would take 100 years for order to be brought back into the Nile valley.

# Conclusion – The Story of the Old Kingdom

Looking back at the roughly 500 years of the Old Kingdom, we are struck by the influence of the educated elites and the families which produced pharaohs. In the beginning, they were a small group in a Bronze Age river valley. Yet, they took control of the wealth and agricultural potential of the Nile by fielding an effective military, harnessing the theology and rituals of the priests, and from their own ranks providing able administrators.

And the rest is history. Quite literally. When Djoser and Imhotep disassembled tradition by building the radically different royal tomb at Saqqara (the Step Pyramid), fierce independence and confidence bordering on hubris swept into the royal families and their ablest elites. In a breathtaking rush, they left us with a collection of massive pyramids that define the Old Kingdom for us. It's what we think of first when we talk about the history of ancient Egypt.

True, the story of the Old Kingdom includes more than the pyramids. There is wonderful art left on their walls and in the temples. The record of international trade, military campaigns in Nubia and Libya, experiments in regional government (which led to the downfall of the Kingdom), fabric and fashion, engineering precision of the highest order, and some simple scientific advances. Still, we sense why and how of all this splendor by considering how the first great pyramids were conceived and built. They were thrown up and made possible by the control and security of the early royal families and the prosperity their policies and religion brought into the Nile valley. The story of the Old Kingdom is the story of the pyramid-building age. And what a fantastic story it is!

# Here's another book by Captivating History that you might like

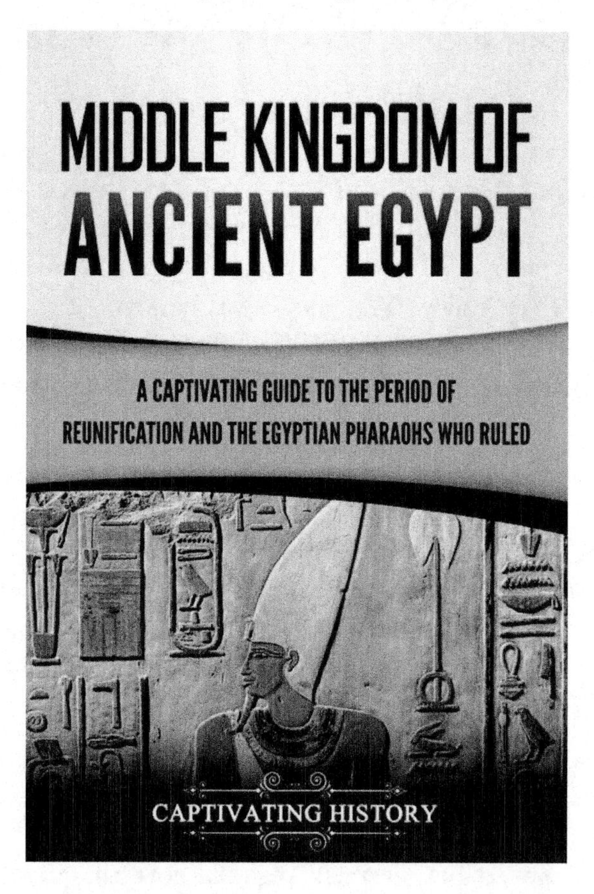

# Free Bonus from Captivating History (Available for a Limited time)

Hi History Lovers!

Now you have a chance to join our exclusive history list so you can get your first history ebook for free as well as discounts and a potential to get more history books for free! Simply visit the link below to join.

Captivatinghistory.com/ebook

Also, make sure to follow us on Facebook, Twitter and Youtube by searching for Captivating History.

# References

The Story of Egypt. Joann Fletcher. Hodder and Stoughton. 2015.

Lives of the Ancient Egyptians. Toby Wilkinson. Thames and Hudson. 2007.

Egypt. The World of the Pharaohs. Edited by Regine Schulz and Matthias Seidel. HF Ullmann.

Printed in Great Britain
by Amazon

16230238R00037